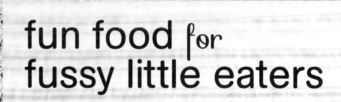

fun food for
fussy little eaters

fun food for fussy little eaters

how to get your kids to eat fruit & veg

Smita Srivastava
of Little Food Junction

photography by William Reavell

RYLAND PETERS & SMALL
LONDON • NEW YORK

Dedication
To my daughter Nandika, thanks to whom
I am an author today!

Author's acknowledgments
Heartfelt thanks to my hubby Siddhartha who is
"always my better half", who has motivated and
encouraged me at every step and spent long
sleepless nights lending the most patient ear to my
wacky dreams and ideas. To my mother, who has
been my inspiration, who prepared some cute salads
for me to munch on almost 2 decades back (Mom,
I still remember your tomato baskets and potato
snowman)! To my father, who taught me to listen
to my heart. To all my dear readers of Little Food
Junction (www.littlefoodjunction.com) who viewed,
liked and commented on my foodie creations.
I owe this book to all of you.

Big thanks to my agent Sallyanne Sweeney and the
staff of RPS for your guidance at every step, for
the untiring efforts all of you have put in. Thanks
for making my dream come true!

Words fall short to convey all the blessings the
Almighty has bestowed upon me; I have felt His
divine presence whenever I needed Him.

Senior Designer Iona Hoyle
Commissioning Editor Céline Hughes
Senior Production Controller Toby Marshall
Editorial Director Julia Charles
Art Director Leslie Harrington

Prop Stylist Lisa Harrison
Food Stylist Maud Eden
Food Stylist's Assistant Natalie Costaras
Indexer Hilary Bird

First published in the UK in 2013
by Ryland Peters & Small
20–21 Jockey's Fields
London WC1R 4BW
and
519 Broadway, 5th Floor
New York, NY 10012
www.rylandpeters.com

10 9 8 7 6 5 4 3 2 1

Text © Smita Srivastava 2013
Design and photographs
© Ryland Peters & Small 2013

ISBN: 978-1-84975-454-5

This is book is intended to provide inspiration for
fun children's mealtimes. Neither the author nor the
publisher can be held responsible for any claim
arising out of the information in this book. Always
consult a health advisor or nutritionist if you have
any concerns about your child's health or nutrition.

A CIP record for this book is available from the
British Library.

A CIP record for this book is available from the
Library of Congress

Printed in China

contents

feed their imaginations

It all started on a bright, sunny day. As usual my little one returned from school with her lunchbox untouched. That evening, her dinner plate met the same fate. Every morsel of food led to endless coaxing and a daily mealtime war. I became so fed up that I tried to think of new ways to get her to eat. Eventually, I shaped the food on her plate into a pair of eyes and a mouth. Soon the room was filled with peals of laughter, and the meal that used to remain on the table for hours vanished in minutes!

The subsequent change in my daughter's eating habits was like magic. These new, creative experiments led me to cleverly disguise regular foods and my fussy little eater was soon trying new fruits and vegetables. Lunchtime turned into fun-time and my daughter was enjoying food again. Her classmates even stood around her desk and applauded as she opened her lunchbox!

My experiment was so rewarding that I decided to share it with other despairing parents in my very own blog: Little Food Junction. In a very short time not only had the ideas won the hearts of families around the world, but news of their success was making its way into national newspapers. Parents were writing in to say that these entertaining recipes had added sparkle to boring mealtimes.

This easy book shows you how to add a little excitement to your child's meals and amaze them with stories on their plates! With an emphasis on fruit and vegetables, the ideas are not only health-giving and visually appealing, but also quick to assemble, so you will end up spending more quality time with your child as well as having fun with them.

The creations that can be carefully wrapped in clingfilm/plastic wrap and taken to school in a box are clearly marked with this lunchbox symbol: ▣ Having said that, use your imagination and adapt ideas to make them more portable if you like.

The ingredients are endlessly adaptable. If your child doesn't like olives, swap them for black grapes. Use radishes instead of carrots, or kiwi instead of cucumber. I would always recommend wholemeal/whole-wheat bread and good cheese, plus seasonal produce when possible.

You don't need fancy gadgets for anything here; you will be well on your way with a knife, some basic cookie cutters and a drinking straw. If you don't have a cookie cutter, use an upturned glass. A cocktail stick/toothpick or skewer is brilliant for cutting shapes out of thin slices of cheese.

Don't throw away any leftovers or off-cuts: use vegetables in salads, soups and stews; fruits for smoothies; and bread for croutons or breadcrumbs.

Use your imagination and get your child to help – and get used to seeing big smiles and empty plates!

fun at the zoo

elephant fruitwich

My daughter is very fond of drawing elephants with long trunks, so I designed this sandwich creation as a homage to her artwork (and a great way to add fruit to her meals).

peanut butter

1 slice of bread

1 black grape, halved crossways

3 slices of kiwi

1 slice of orange, skin on

1 banana

round cookie cutter, no wider than the slice of bread

knife

1

Spread some peanut butter neatly on the slice of bread. Cut the bread with the cookie cutter.

2

Put 1 grape half, cut side down, on a kiwi slice. Put these on the bread slice for eyes.

3

Cut the orange slice into 2 half moons. Place above the bread as ears. Cut the last kiwi slice into 2 half moons. Place 1 half, straight side uppermost, as a mouth.

4

Cut the banana in half lengthwise to make a trunk. Chop a bit off if it is too long. Place on the elephant face so that it bends away from the face.

friendly lion

The large mane of the lion has always fascinated my daughter so when I was inventing this food art, I tried to emphasize the gorgeous mane. The carrots can be substituted with shavings of yellow courgette/zucchini if you like.

1 slice of cheese

1 slice of bread

1 large carrot

1 small pickled gherkin

2 black pitted olives

round plain cookie cutter and round, fluted cookie cutter, no wider than the slice of cheese or bread

grater

knife

Cut the cheese into a circle with the fluted cookie cutter. Cut the slice of bread with the round cookie cutter. Lay the cheese on the bread.

Grate the carrot and arrange it all the way around the bread/cheese circles. Snip any longer pieces of carrot to make them all roughly the same length.

Cut 4 thin slices from the gherkin. Cut the remaining gherkin lengthways into 6 matchsticks. Cut 1 olive in half crossways. Cut 1 olive in half lengthways.

Cut 1 long olive half in half crossways. Cut off a half-moon slice from 1 piece. Arrange all the pieces of olive and gherkin on the face, and as ears and paws.

nosy fox

A clever little fox, hidden among the bushes, is the perfect basis for a tiny tot story. Every time I narrate one of these stories to my little one, she thrusts out her lips to exaggerate the letter "O" in "fox" and its long snout.

1 slice of cheese

1 slice of bread

2 equal slices of strawberry, cut lengthways

2 slices of cucumber

2 black pitted olives

2 sprigs of fresh dill

1 frilly lettuce leaf

1 green blade of spring onion/scallion

a few peas, blanched

round cookie cutter

knife

Lay the cheese on the bread. Cut the bottom 2 corners off using the cookie cutter. Use the strawberry slices as ears in the top 2 corners of the bread.

Use the cucumber slices as eyes. Cut 1 olive in half crossways. Place 1 on the top left of each cucumber slice, cut side down.

Use the whole olive horizontally for the nose. Place a dill sprig horizontally in each side of the nose, through the hole in the olive to hold them in place.

Tear the lettuce into little pieces. Cut the onion into 2–3 lengths and make into trees, dotted with peas. Arrange the lettuce along the bottom as grass.

croissant crab

When my daughter was a tiny toddler, it was difficult for her to pronounce the word "croissant", so at each visit to the bakery, she used to call it a "crab". Then, one day, I decided to add some eyes and claws to make it come alive.

4 slices of cucumber

1 curved croissant

finely snipped chive

5 small sprigs of fresh dill

1 black pitted olive, halved lengthways

2 slices of radish

3 slices of carrot

2 nigella/onion seeds

knife

tiny round cookie cutter

1

Cut a wedge out of 2 cucumber slices. Place 1 slice on each point of the croissant. Arrange chive bubbles around and dill seaweed along the bottom.

2

Put 1 olive half, cut side down, on a radish slice and stack it on a whole cucumber slice. Use each stack as an eye on the croissant crab.

3

Using the cookie cutter, stamp through 1 carrot slice to make a teardrop and a crescent. Use the crescent as a mouth.

4

Cut 2 wedges out of 2 whole carrot slices to make fish bodies. The wedges will become tails. Arrange above the crab and finish with nigella seeds for eyes.

blushing raccoon

We spotted a raccoon for the first time at the local zoo and since then my little one has loved its eye patch and jokingly calls it the raccoon's spectacles. This raccoon sandwich is not only cute but also perfect for cheese fans.

1 slice of bread

1 slice of cheese

2 slices of radish

2 black pitted olives

3 slices of cucumber

2 drops of tomato sauce

1 sprig of parsley, stalk included

round cookie cutter, no wider than the slice of bread

cocktail stick/toothpick

knife

Cut the bread and cheese with the cookie cutter. Using the cocktail stick/toothpick, cut a wavy mask shape out of the cheese. Gently lift it onto the bread.

Cut 1 olive in half lengthways. Place 1 half, cut side down, on each radish slice. Use as eyes. Cut 1 olive in half crossways. Use as a nose. Cut a half-moon olive slice for a mouth.

Cut 1 cucumber slice in half. Cut the tip from each half and use as ears. Put a drop of tomato sauce on each cheek.

Dice the remaining cucumber for a treetop. Use the parsley stalk for the tree trunk and the sprigs for grass.

slithery snake

Toddlers around the world learn that snakes slither in a wavy motion. My daughter loves oranges and they're perfect for depicting the slithery movement of an agile snake, but you could use kiwis instead to ring the changes.

4–5 black pitted olives

2 equal slices of strawberry, cut crossways

4 slices of cucumber

4 slices of orange, skin on

1 thin length of red (bell) pepper

1 frilly lettuce leaf, torn into pieces

knife

tiny round cookie cutter

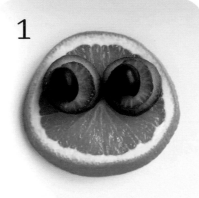

1

Cut 1 olive in half lengthways. Put 1 olive half, cut side down, on a strawberry slice and stack it on a cucumber slice. Use as eyes on an orange slice.

2

Cut 2 orange slices into half moons. Cut 1 orange slice into quarters. Cut 3–4 olives into slices. Cut the pepper into a forked tongue shape. Cut 1 cucumber slice in half.

3

Place an orange quarter against the face, then 4 half moons in alternate directions, then an orange quarter. Cut a moon from 1 cucumber slice with the cookie cutter.

4

Arrange the lettuce along the bottom. Finish with a cucumber half-moon mouth, olive-slice scales and pepper tongue.

fairy tales

the princess and the frog

My daughter likes this fairy tale, especially the part when the princess kisses the frog and it turns into a handsome prince. When I make this food art for her, she gobbles up the necklace and the crown first.

1 slice of bread

1 carrot

1 black pitted olive, halved lengthways

2 slices of cucumber

1 small piece of red (bell) pepper

2 drops of tomato sauce

1/4 yellow (bell) pepper

1 slice of kiwi

8 corn kernels, blanched

1 black grape, halved crossways

spinach leaf and grape "water lilies" (optional)

round cookie cutter

julienne peeler/grater

knife

Cut the bread with the cookie cutter. Julienne/grate the carrot. Place around the bread to make hair.

Place 1 olive half, cut side down, on each cucumber slice. Use as eyes. Cut a mouth from the red pepper. Put a drop of tomato sauce on each cheek.

Cut a small square from the yellow pepper. Cut out tiny triangles from the top to make a crown. Do the same with a smaller square of pepper for the frog's crown.

Cut a large wedge from the kiwi slice. Add 2 grape halves and a crown to make a frog. Put the larger crown on the princess' head and make a necklace from the corn.

bell the cat

This edible version of the fable fills my house with tons of laughter and giggles. The little one says "I know the easiest solution to the mice's problems" and quickly eats up the croissant cat!

1 curved croissant

4 slices of cucumber

2 black pitted olives, halved lengthways

2 large slices of carrot, cut into half moons

4 chives

1/2 radish

1 tiny slice of cheese

knife

drinking straw (optional)

Position the croissant pointed sides up. Cut a large wedge from 2 cucumber slices. Place 1 wedge on each point of the croissant. Cut 4 half slices from 1 olive half.

Put a carrot half moon on each whole slice of cucumber. Arrange an olive half on each slice. Use as eyes. Use an olive half as a nose and 2 olive half slices as a mouth.

Place 3 chives horizontally through the hole in the olive to hold them in place. Trim the radish half to look like a bell. Put the remaining olive quarter under the bell.

Make 2 mice with 2 carrot half moons, 2 olive half slices, chive legs and long chive tails. Using the straw, stamp 4 tiny circles from the cheese for the cat and mice eyes.

tom thumb snacks

Kids are very fond of itsy bitsy tiny edibles and these crackers are the perfect excuse for a quick nibble. Use some peanut butter or mayonnaise as edible glue if you intend to make these for a lunchbox or a party.

2 slices of cheese

2 crackers

1 slice of cucumber, cut into half moons

1 very small slice of firm tomato (preferably seedless), cut into half moons

6 peas, blanched

1 small sprig of parsley

nigella/onion seeds

flower-shaped cookie cutter, no wider than the cheese or crackers

knife

1

Cut the slices of cheese with the cookie cutter. (Keep any leftover cheese to chop up and sprinkle over soups.)

2

Lay the cheese slices on the crackers. (Stick them down with mayonnaise or peanut butter if you want to transport the snacks.)

3

Lay the cucumber half moons on 1 cheese slice and top neatly with the tomato half moons.

4

Arrange the peas in a triangle on the other cheese slice. Garnish with the parsley sprig. Arrange the nigella seeds in a curve on the tomato half moons.

rapunzel lunch

This lunch fascinates my daughter, who is so fond of long hair. I often use tomato and spinach-flavoured spaghetti to give Rapunzel a modern makeover.

1 portion cooked wholemeal/whole-wheat spaghetti

1 bowl of thick tomato soup

5 slices of baby corn, blanched

5 parsley stalks

1 piece of toast

1 black pitted olive, halved lengthways

2 slices of radish

2 slices of carrot

1 small piece of red (bell) pepper

1 frilly lettuce leaf

tiny round cookie cutter

knife

Arrange the spaghetti above and along one side of the bowl of soup to make hair. Position the corn and parsley stalks as flowers at the bottom of the plate.

Cut out 2 circles from the toast using the cookie cutter. Put 1 olive half on each circle of toast as eyes.

Using the cookie cutter, stamp through 1 carrot slice to make a teardrop and a crescent. Use the crescent as a mouth. Cut 2 triangles from the pepper for a bow.

Arrange the lettuce as a dress. Put the bow on the hair. Cut the carrot teardrop into triangles and place with 1 carrot slice as the sun. Put the features on the soup last.

pinocchio on my plate

Pinocchio's ever-growing nose makes such a sweet story. My daughter eats the corn nose, then turns Pinocchio's mouth upside down and says, "He's sad because he cannot lie any more for he has no nose."

1 slice of cheese

1 slice of bread

1 small cucumber

1 black pitted olive, halved crossways

1 cherry tomato, halved

1 frilly lettuce leaf

1 slice of radish

1 small piece of yellow (bell) pepper

3 peas, blanched

1 baby corn, blanched

2 parsley stalks

round plain cookie cutter, no wider than the slice of cheese or bread

knife

tiny round cookie cutter

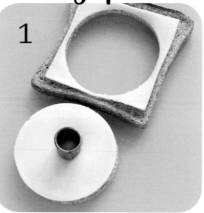

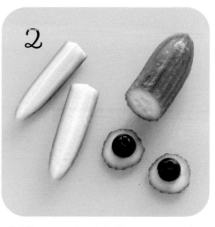

Lay the cheese on top of the bread. Cut a circle through both using the larger cookie cutter. Cut out a circle for the nose in the centre with the tiny cutter.

Cut the cucumber in half crossways. Cut 2 slices from 1 half and top with the olive halves for eyes. Cut the other cucumber lengthways into quarters for the arms.

Arrange the eyes, tomato cheeks and lettuce hair on the face. Cut a half moon from the radish slice and use as a mouth. Cut the pepper into 2 equal triangles.

Arrange the pepper bow and pea buttons under the face. Put the cucumber arms and corn nose in place. Use the parsley stalks for puppet strings.

three little pigs

When I declare "3 little piggies: here comes Nandika the Wolfie", my daughter Nandika makes a loud scary howling noise and starts eating the orange piggies.

1 small cucumber

3 slices of orange (preferably of varying sizes), skin on

6 peas, blanched

3 black grapes, halved crossways

3 beet(root) sprouts

5 baby spinach leaves

4 chives

knife

Cut 6 slices from the cucumber – try to get 1 larger slice for a bigger pair of ears. Cut this bigger slice plus 2 of the others into half moons.

Place 1 small cucumber slice on each orange slice. Cut 3 peas in half and place 2 halves, cut side down, on each cucumber slice for nostrils.

Arrange 2 cucumber half moons at the top of each orange slice as ears.

Add 2 grape halves, cut side down, to each piggie for eyes. Give each piggie a sprout tail. Decorate the scene with spinach-leaf and chive trees.

happy holidays

easter chick salad

This fresh, vibrant salad adds zing to the Easter holidays. My little one loves to save the chick to last, and munches on the broccoli trees and crunchy sun first.

2 big tablespoons corn
    kernels, blanched

3 slices of carrot

1 strip of red (bell) pepper

1 black pitted olive,
    halved crossways

1 strawberry, halved
    lengthways

4 broccoli florets, steamed

round cookie cutter

knife

Put the cookie cutter on the serving plate and scatter all but 13 of the corn kernels neatly inside it. Gently lift the cutter away without disturbing the corn.

Take 2 carrot slices. Cut 2 wedges out of each of them, then place under the corn for feet. Arrange the remaining corn kernels around the last carrot slice for a sun.

Cut a triangle from the strip of pepper to make a beak. Place it, pointing down, on the corn circle and position the olive halves, cut side down, above as eyes.

Cut 2 wedges from the wide end of the strawberry slice and place above the corn circle for a tuft of fur. Arrange the broccoli trees on either side of the chick.

fruity halloween eyeballs

Instead of pampering my daughter and her friends with sugar-laden sweets on Halloween, I love treating them to yummy, crunchy power-boosting fruit "eyeballs" before they go out trick-or-treating.

1 small red apple

bowl of cold water with ¹/₂ teaspoon lemon juice

1 strawberry

2 slices of kiwi

1 black grape, halved crossways

1 grape and parsley-stalk "spider" (optional)

apple corer

knife

Core the apple. Cut it in half across the middle (the 2 halves don't have to be equal) and dip the cut sides in the lemony water to stop them browning.

Cut 2 slices crossways from the strawberry. Now cut 10 thin strips from the rest of the strawberry. They should be about the length of the slices.

Cut the ends off the 2 apple halves to make a level surface if they aren't steady. Place a kiwi slice on each cut side of the apple halves.

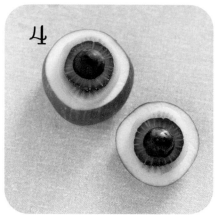

Put 1 grape half, cut side down, on a strawberry slice and stack it on a kiwi slice. Put 5 strawberry strips around the eyes, from the grape to the edge of the apple.

smiling jack-o-lantern

This sandwich is fun to make. I usually get all the ingredients cut and ready on a plate and then ask my daughter to assemble it. She loves it! If you like, you can spread peanut butter or whatever's liked on the bread before topping with the carrots.

- 1 slice of bread
- ½ carrot
- 1 slice of beet(root), steamed
- 2 green grapes, halved lengthways
- 2 half-grape and parsley-stalk spiders (optional)

round cookie cutter

knife

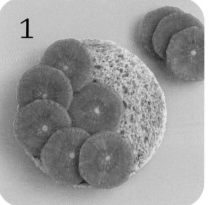

Cut the bread with the cookie cutter. Cut about 10 slices from the carrot and arrange neatly over the bread slice.

Cut the beet(root) slice into a half moon. Cut 2 wedges out of 1 half moon to make a mouth. Position on the carrot face.

Cut the other beet(root) half moon into 2 equal triangles and position above the mouth as eyes.

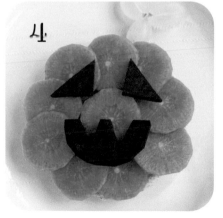

Arrange the grapes above the jack-o-lantern as a stalk.

thanksgiving turkey

The skewered-grape feathers on this Thanksgiving turkey are so clever. Put this creation on a plastic plate or box lid, wrap it carefully in clingfilm/plastic wrap, and it will happily travel in a lunchbox. Or the skewers can be eaten on the go!

1 slice of bread

peanut butter

7 black grapes

9 green grapes

1 thick slice of apple, dipped in a bowl of cold water with ½ teaspoon lemon juice

1 small slice of orange

1 strawberry, halved lengthways

2–3 sprigs of parsley, stalk included

round cookie cutter

knife

5 toothpicks/cocktail sticks

Cut the bread with the cookie cutter. Reserve the off-cuts. Spread some peanut butter on the bread. Cut 1 black grape in half crossways and set aside.

Spear 3 grapes on each cocktail stick/toothpick, leaving a little space on the ends of the sticks. Push the sticks side by side around the edge of the apple slice in a fan.

Put the apple slice on top of the bread, above centre. Stack with the orange slice and finish with the 2 reserved grape halves for the eyes.

Cut the strawberry slice into 3 wedges and use the neatest one as a beak. Cut 2 dice from the bread off-cuts and use as feet. Decorate with parsley trees.

santa sandwich

Christmas isn't complete without Santa and soon your Christmas won't be the same without a Santa sandwich! My little one is very fond of cherry tomatoes, so I created this design to make the most of these festive red treasures.

2 slices of cheese

1 slice of bread

1 black pitted olive, halved crossways

4 cherry tomatoes, halved

3 slices of cucumber, cut into half moons

1 green blade of spring onion/scallion

2 red-(bell)-pepper stars (optional)

knife

flower-shaped cookie cutter and round plain cookie cutter, no wider than the slice of cheese or bread

drinking straw

Cut 1 cheese slice with the flower cookie cutter. Now cut into it with the round cutter to leave behind a beard shape. Cut the slice of bread with the round cutter.

Place the cheese beard on the bottom half of the bread. Cut a half slice from 1 olive half and use as a mouth. Use the 2 olive halves for eyes.

Place 1 tomato half, cut side down, on the face for a nose. Arrange the others, cut side up, in a triangle for a hat. Put the cucumber half moons in a tree shape.

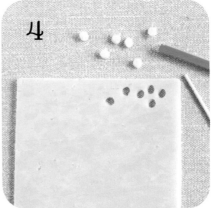

Using the straw, stamp tiny circles from the cheese for snowflakes. Cut a strip from the cheese as a band for Santa's hat. Finish the tree with an onion trunk.

tropical christmas tree

This was my way of thanking my daughter for the Christmas card she made me by sticking together green semi-circles and red sequins. Make a veggie version by replacing the kiwi with cucumber halves and a red-(bell)-pepper-star (see page 40).

4 kiwi slices

1 strawberry, halved lengthways

8 pomegranate seeds

2 slices of banana, dipped in a bowl of cold water with $\frac{1}{2}$ teaspoon lemon juice

2 green grapes, halved lengthways

knife

tiny star-shaped cookie cutter

1

Cut the kiwi slices into half moons. Cut the banana slices into half moons.

2

Arrange the kiwi half moons in 2 columns to look like a tree.

3

Stamp out a star from the strawberry using the cookie cutter.

4

Place the pomegranate seeds on the kiwi tips. Top with the strawberry star. Lay the grape halves down the length of the tree. Finish with 3 banana half moons for a pot.

nature all around

curly caterpillar

I usually serve Nandika's favourite sunny-side-up eggs with lots of salad. One day, we had just come in from the garden, so what could be better than letting the caterpillars we saw there make their way onto our plates…

a drop of vegetable oil

1 slice/ring of red (bell) pepper

1 egg

1 black pitted olive, halved lengthways

9 slices of cucumber

2 French beans, raw or blanched

tomato sauce

1 frilly lettuce leaf, torn into pieces

frying pan

fish slice/spatula

knife

1

Heat a drop of oil in the frying pan. Place the pepper in the pan and gently break the egg into it. Cook until the egg is set to your child's liking.

2

Carefully transfer the pepper-egg to a plate using a fish slice/spatula. Cut a half slice from 1 olive half and set aside. Use the 2 olive halves as eyes.

3

Trim 1 slice of cucumber so that it fits snugly up against the pepper ring. Overlap the remaining slices to make a curly caterpillar body.

4

Make a mouth with the reserved olive half slice. Add the beans for antennae. Put a drop of tomato sauce on each cheek. Arrange the lettuce along the bottom.

hello birdie

My daughter is very fond of the birdhouse that we made together some time back. While the original stands perched in the garden, this edible one often makes its way to her little tummy.

1 slice of bread

1 black pitted olive, halved crossways

1 slice of cheese

12 corn kernels, blanched

2 slices of carrot

1 small cucumber, cut into 5 strips using a mandoline or vegetable peeler

1 frilly lettuce leaf, torn into pieces

2 nigella/onion seeds

knife

drinking straw

Cut the crusts from the slice of bread and set them aside. Cut 4 half slices from 1 olive half to make 2 flying birds.

Lay the slice of cheese on the bread. Cut the top 2 corners off to make a roof. Using the straw, stamp 2 tiny circles from the leftover cheese. Cut out a tiny triangle too.

Arrange the reserved bread crusts over the roof, under the house, and as a pole, trimming them to fit. Arrange the corn kernels around 1 carrot slice for a sun.

Arrange the cucumber plants and lettuce grass. Put 1 carrot slice on the house and top with the olive half. Make a face from the tiny cheese pieces and eyes from the seeds.

sunny day

A brightly shining sun and puffy, pillowy clouds are things that I love to recreate on a plate on a gloriously sunny day. The first thing my little one picks up from it has to be the sun's juicy, puffy cheeks.

1 slice of bread

1 carrot

1–2 slices of cheese

2 black pitted olives, halved lengthways

1 cherry tomato, halved

1 tiny piece of baby corn, blanched

tomato sauce

2 tiny lengths of parsley stalk

round cookie cutter

knife

tiny round cookie cutter

Cut the bread with the larger cookie cutter. Cut 9 slices from the carrot. Cut 7 of the slices into half moons and arrange 13 of them all the way around the bread.

Cut 16 circles from the cheese, using the tiny cookie cutter. Arrange 14 in clusters as clouds. Cut a tiny triangle from 1 carrot half moon and 2 tiny blobs from an olive half.

Use 2 carrot slices and 2 olive halves to make eyes. Using the tiny cutter, stamp through 2 cheese circles to make 2 teardrops and crescents.

Make tomato cheeks, a corn nose and sauce mouth. Make a bird from 1 cheese teardop and 2 crescents, the tiny carrot and olive pieces and the parsley stalks.

flower garden

This is an edible replica of the card that my daughter and I made together to wish her grandparents a happy spring. And surely nothing could reflect spring more strongly than blooming flowers – that are good enough to eat!

1 slice of orange, skin on

about 10 blueberries

1 small piece of carrot

4–5 strawberries

6 tiny lengths of parsley stalk

2 French beans, raw or blanched and cut into 4 different lengths

2 green grapes, halved lengthways

knife

1

Top the orange slice with about 7 blueberries. Cut the carrot into equal matchsticks about the length of the strawberries.

2

Cut about 9 equal slices, lengthways, from the strawberries. Arrange them all around the orange slice. Cut 3 slices crossways from a strawberry.

3

Lay 1 carrot matchstick along the centre of each strawberry petal. Cut the pointed bottom off 1 strawberry and use as a little bug with parsley-stalk legs.

4

Put a blueberry on each round strawberry round. Add the beans as flower stems and garnish with grape halves or quarters for leaves.

night owl

We used to have a big tree just outside our old house. Often, during late evenings, my daughter used to sit near the window facing it to catch a glimpse of the owl who used to hoot all through the night.

2 slices of orange,
  1 slightly smaller
  than the other, skin on

¹/₄ cucumber

2–3 black pitted olives,
  halved crossways

2 slices of strawberry,
  cut crossways

1 slice of kiwi, cut into
  half moons

4–5 green grapes, halved
  lengthways

knife

tiny round cookie cutter

Overlap the smaller orange slice on the larger one to make the owl's body. Cut 1 slice of cucumber. Cut a moon from it with the cookie cutter.

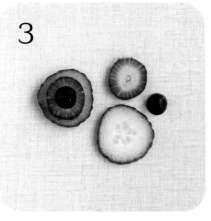

Cut 2 slices of cucumber for the eyes. Cut out a triangle and 2 sets of matchsticks, of varying lengths, from the remaining piece to make the beak and head feathers.

Put 1 olive half, cut side down, on a strawberry slice and stack it on a cucumber slice. Use as eyes on the smaller orange slice.

Arrange the beak, feathers and kiwi wings on the owl. Cut the olive halves into half slices and use for the belly and feet. Use grape halves and quarters for a branch.

party time

flower pops

Any food on a stick seems to appeal to children, so I made these healthy "pops" for a spring party at our home and they were the first things to get gobbled up.

1–2 large slices of watermelon

3–4 small black grapes

a few green grapes

1 frilly lettuce leaf

flower-shaped cookie cutter

tiny round cookie cutter

3–4 skewers

1 small bowl or glass, to hold the "flowers"

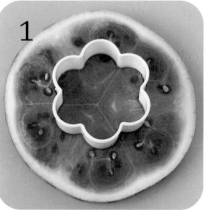

Remove any black seeds from the watermelon if necessary. Cut as many flowers out of the watermelon as you can/like using the flower cutter.

Using the tiny cutter, stamp out a hole in the centre of each flower.

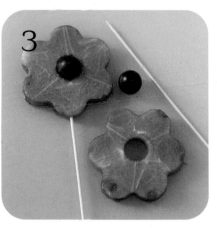

Put a black grape in each hole and push the skewer all the way up the middle of the watermelon and grape. Stop before the stick pokes out of the top of the flower.

Push the green grapes onto the skewers to make flower stems. Trim the sharp ends of the skewers before handing to children. Arrange in a bowl filled with lettuce.

party peacock

My daughter adores peacocks – she even has a few peacock feathers in her room. When her friends come over to play and I want to serve them a snack, I love to make them a party peacock!

½ apple, dipped in a bowl of cold water with ½ teaspoon lemon juice

5 kiwi slices

2 chocolate chips

2 small cookies

1 small handful of rocket/ arugula leaves

knife

drinking straw

Cut the apple half into 2 quarters and set 1 aside. Core the other quarter and cut it into 9 slim slices. Dip the slices in the lemony water to stop them browning.

Cut the kiwi slices into half moons. Using the straw, stamp 2 tiny circles from a thin piece of the remaining apple quarter to make eyes. Top each with a chocolate chip.

Put the cookies, one above the other, on a plate and arrange the apple slices in a fan around them. Put the kiwi half moons on top of the apple slices.

Cut a triangle and 4 matchsticks from the apple to make a beak, head feathers and legs. Place the apple-chocolate eyes. Finish with rocket/arugula leaves for grass.

pirate boats

These tiny appetizers were a hit at a kids party. I had placed some hollow tomato halves, 3 types of fillings and pepper sails on a large platter and the kids had a chance to get involved and make a boat of their liking.

2 firm tomatoes

fillings of your choice, eg. herbed cream cheese, coleslaw, cress, egg mayonnaise

medium pieces of yellow and green (bell) peppers

shredded red cabbage

1 fat slice of cucumber, cut into half moons

knife

spoon

3 cocktail sticks/ toothpicks

2 miniature flags on sticks

Cut the tomatoes in half and carefully scoop the seeds out.

Fill the hollow tomato cups with your choice of filling.

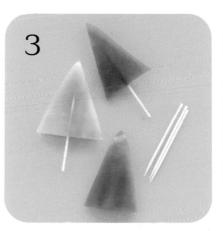

Cut 3 triangles out of the peppers. Push a cocktail stick/toothpick up through each one vertically. Push 1 upright into each tomato boat through the filling.

Fill a plate with shredded red cabbage as sea water. Top with the boats. Push the miniature flags into the cucumber half moons and stand these little boats upright.

fishy fun

The theme at a recent summer vacation party was "let's go fishing" and the games revolved around catching artificial fish from a large water tub. We made these cute sandwiches too as they're quick to assemble.

2 slices of bread

2 slices of cheese

1 black pitted olive, halved crossways

5 slices of cucumber

2 slices of carrot, cut into half moons

tomato sauce

finely snipped spring onion/scallion

round plain cookie cutter, no wider than the slice of cheese or bread

knife

1

Cut the 2 bread slices with the cookie cutter. Cut the 2 cheese slices with the cookie cutter.

2

Lay each slice of cheese directly on a slice of bread.

3

Cut 2 half slices from 1 olive half and use as mouths. Top 2 slices of cucumber with an olive half for eyes. Cut 3 cucumber slices into half moons for scales.

4

Arrange 3 cucumber half moons as scales and 2 carrot half moons as tails. Put a drop of tomato sauce on each cheek. Place the onion slices around as bubbles.

fairy toadstool

An alfresco summer party requires a lot of arrangements, so it helps if the children's food is easy to make, as well as healthy. These toadstools fit the bill and little hands will enjoy adding the cress grass and applying the cheesy dots.

thick-cut half moon from a small watermelon

1 small cucumber

1 slice of cheese

1 handful of cress

1 frilly lettuce leaf, torn into pieces

1 black grape, quartered

1 tiny length of parsley stalk

knife

tiny round cookie cutter

1

Remove any black seeds from the watermelon if necessary. Place on a plate, curved side uppermost.

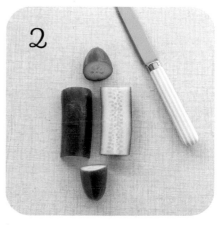

2

Trim the ends of the cucumber. Cut the cucumber in half vertically. Put 1 cucumber half, vertically and cut side down, under the watermelon as a stem.

3

Cut out about 6 circles from the cheese using the cookie cutter. Place them on the watermelon and trim the circles to fit within the contours of the watermelon.

4

Place some cress soil and lettuce grass under the toadstool. Make a butterfly with 4 grape quarters topped with the tiny parsley stalk.

index

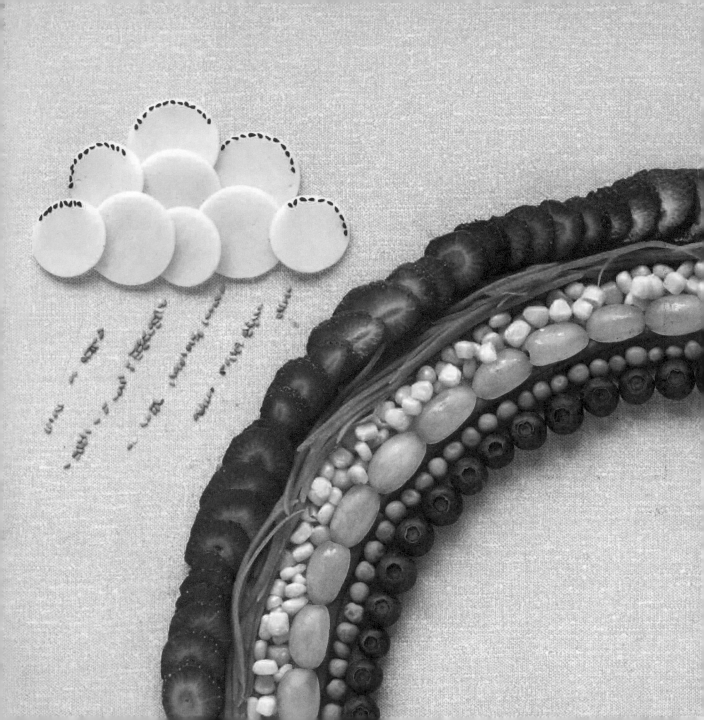